Back

French Inspired Bench

side.

leg detail

Side

SUZANNE KASLER
INSPIRED INTERIORS

SUZANNE KASLER
INSPIRED INTERIORS

WRITTEN WITH CHRISTINE PITTEL, DESIGNED BY DOUG TURSHEN WITH DAVID HUANG

RIZZOLI
NEW YORK

Acknowledgments

First, I would like to thank my family: my darling husband, John Morris, and adorable daughter, Alexandra, who have always supported my work and to whom this book is dedicated; my parents, James and Martha Kasler, who always encouraged me to pursue my dreams of design; and all of my family, friends, and colleagues who have touched my life and work immeasurably.

Special thanks also go to my clients who let me do such beautiful work, without whom this book would not be possible; my fabulous and talented office, without whom this beautiful work would not be done; and every magazine and editor kind enough to publish and encourage my work, including *Atlanta Homes & Lifestyles, Architectural Digest, Benjamin Moore Color, Coastal Living, Elle Decor, House & Garden, House Beautiful, Southern Accents, Traditional Home,* and *Veranda.*

And to everyone who has touched this book in some way—to all of the photographers who have captured the essence of my design with such poignant elegance; to Jill Cohen who brought me to Rizzoli; to Sandy Gilbert and everyone at Rizzoli for publishing my work and creating some of the most fabulous books ever; to Doug Turshen, whose brilliant eye has produced a book that seamlessly reflects my style; to Christine Pittel, whose amazing pen has captured my voice; to Janie Wilburn, whose creative efforts have helped this book come to fruition; and to everyone and everything that has inspired me over time to create such inspired interiors.

Contents

Introduction

I'M ALWAYS LOOKING. Ever since I can remember, I've been aware of my surroundings, noticing things like the profile of a molding or the fall of a curtain. I always tell my staff that I'm constantly working—and, in fact, it's true. Everything around me is inspiration. The other night at a restaurant, a big wooden bowl of forsythia caught my eye. There was something about the yellow against the dark wood and the proportions of the branches to the vase that interested me, and I filed it away in my mental bank of images. Shopping with my daughter for a dress, I may come across an unusual pleat that could translate into a detail on a slipcover. I live and breathe design.

Design can make a difference. When a client asks me to do a house, the process is about more than decoration. It's about showing people how to live better and enjoy their own home. I ask a lot of questions and listen carefully to their answers, because then I can figure out exactly what they need. A mudroom with lockers for the children, a dog door in the laundry, French doors leading from the breakfast room to the terrace—these are the kinds of things that make life easier.

I want my clients to love their houses. As I tell them, you should have one thing in each room that's special to you, and often, this special object inspires the design direction. It can be a painting found at an antiques shop or a quirky piece of furniture or a collection of photographs—what matters is that it means something to you. In a house that works, each member of the family finds his own special spot. For my husband, John, it's the library. My daughter, Alexandra, is always at the desk in the sitting room. For me, my favorite space is my bed. At the end of the day, I'll be sitting there, reading messages on my  BlackBerry and thumbing through my magazines, which are stacked within arm's reach. This is how I relax and unwind. But I can't stop thinking about my work. I often wake up in the middle of the night and jot down a note about a call I must make, or a solution to some design problem that I dreamt about.

Design is my passion. I love furniture and objects and that extraordinary thrill you get when you put them together in just the right, unexpected way. People respond to my enthusiasm, and I enjoy sharing my ideas. Being able to work as a designer is a gift—an amazing opportunity to connect to people and design spaces that inspire them.

PART I

AT HOME

At Home

I'VE NEVER PUT A LABEL ON MY STYLE. Why even try to pin it down when there are so many possibilities to explore? I can do traditional or contemporary, sophisticated or casual, high or low—sometimes all in the same room. If a client calls and says she's found something she really likes, I'll say, "Get it." And I will make it work. One of the pleasures of doing a home is expressing your personality. My own home is a collection of all sorts of things that I've been drawn to. No one else would put them together—but that's what creating your own style is all about.

Fifteen years ago, when my husband and I moved to Atlanta with our daughter, I must have looked at 150 houses to buy. Nothing seemed quite right. So we found a lot and decided to build a simple, classical house. I worked very closely with the architects on the design. If you can get the architecture right, it gives you such freedom when you're designing the interiors. There's nothing to compensate for or disguise. This is a two-story, four-bedroom house and the public rooms flow gracefully into each other. They are beautiful in their proportions, with lofty 10-foot ceilings.

An entryway is usually thought of as a space that you just pass through, but mine is different. It's actually furnished so you could sit down and have a conversation. It feels very welcoming. The furniture may be antique but it's far from stuffy, with polka dots on the chair and pink leather on the stool—a color that will reappear in other rooms. The painting is by Steven Seinberg.

One idea I had was to take all the windows down to the ground, which changes the whole feeling of a room. You get much more light, and suddenly the house becomes more European.

I'm very attracted to that continental look. I love the whole French culture—the art, the fashion, the food, the furnishings. In our entryway, I installed a French limestone floor and had the walls painted to look like stone. I found an elegant Louis XVI bench and a little gueridon table in a classic matte-gold finish. There's something so appealing about the lustrous gold against the paleness of the white walls and floor.

White is my signature. In the living room, the walls, ceiling, curtains, carpet, sofas, and mantel are all in shades of white, from milk to cream to taupe. I don't try to match; I just layer them. White is crisp and clean, allowing other colors such as the gray-blue, burnt orange, and greenish-gold on the pillows and the stools to stand out. I'm fascinated by the way even a little bit of color can create a big impression.

With all the whites from floor to ceiling, there's an ethereal quality to the living room. Round acrylic tables by Nancy Corzine almost disappear. I found the two Russian stools in Paris, and made my own stripe out of two different fabrics to cover them. They add character, and extra seating, to the room. I like their shape so much that they inspired the Anastasia bench in my furniture line for Hickory Chair.

There's an unpredictable mix of objects in the family room and it starts with an amazing table from the Van Cleef estate. It really is made of horns and zebra hide. As soon as I saw it in a local antiques shop, I knew I had to have it. I even had it picked up right away, before the dealer could change his mind. It's the kind of special piece that usually takes years to find. The table elevates the whole room to another level. The tapestry hanging over it adds an old-world note, and then there's that burst of orange leather on the chair. I wasn't even sure I liked orange when I saw it sitting all by itself at the Paris flea market, but it was too fabulous to leave behind.

In the dining room, the giant credenza painted in layer after layer of chalky taupe and pink inspired all the colors in the room, including the taupe walls and the pink silk curtains. It's not the same pink that I used on the leather bench in the entryway, because it changes depending on the material. Yet it's similar. It makes you think back to where you've been, while you're wondering what comes next. I think the repetition of certain colors subtly connects the rooms in a house and helps the flow. In a sense, decorating for me is a little like composing music. I'll introduce a theme and then you'll hear it again in another room in a slightly different way. The colors I love carry you through the house. White may be dominant, but it's the pink and the orange and the blue that you remember.

Instead of the typical banisters and newel post, we did a metal railing on the stairs, which feels very French Moderne. The runner is banded in white, to give it a nice tailored edge. The pink leather stools can migrate wherever they're needed. The art over the staircase is special to me. Over the years, I've collected small prints—some black and white, some sepia, some in muted colors—and framed them all differently. I hung them randomly to create interest. The walls are painted in a favorite creamy white—Benjamin Moore's Linen White.

I lined the pink
taffeta curtains
in a platinum-
colored taffeta,
thinking that
I could always
reverse them if I
got tired of the
pink. But that's
never happened.

The café au lait upholstery on the French settee is trimmed
with pink grosgrain ribbon studded with nail heads.

RIGHT: I took the pink and the taupe from the painted finish
on the credenza against the back wall and used those colors
throughout the room. The stripe on the chairs picks up
both shades, but is not an exact match. The antique crystal
chandelier over the table is by Jansen.

When I look at that tapestry, I remember exactly where I was when I found it. I was scouring the Paris flea market for treasures when I spotted it folded up on a bench.

I opened the tapestry up and thought it was beautiful. Usually you sign a slip of paper and your shipper eventually picks up your purchase, but I didn't want to let this tapestry out of my sight. I carried it home with me on the plane. I'm told it was made in the seventeenth century. The bronze-and-resin sconces, shaped like a tortoiseshell, were made in the 1940s. The orange leather chair led to the orange Hermès tray and then the cognac-colored lamps. I think the turquoise-blue Venetian goblet and books are the perfect complement because the turquoise blue is the same value as the orange.

This mirrored vanity is a very pretty piece, which looks even more glamorous against a mirrored wall. Mirroring is a simple detail that does so much to reflect light and create depth. You feel as if the dressing room is suddenly much larger. The ceiling is painted with a platinum metallic paint, which enhances the reflective quality.

RIGHT: The master bedroom began with that beautiful chinoiserie bed by Rose Tarlow. It has such a strong shape against the white walls. I upholstered the headboard in ivory *matelasse* and had custom linens made to continue the play of black and white. The pillows are embroidered with a camellia—a favorite Chanel motif—and the white curtains are trimmed in black grosgrain ribbon, which is also very Chanel. I love to personalize a space with dressmaker details. The geometric fabric on the bench ties all the themes in the room together.

PART II
PRINCIPLES

Classic Elegance

I HAVE GREAT RESPECT FOR TRADITION, and I like doing traditional interiors. But I always try to find a fresh approach that suits the way we live today. Just because a house is traditional doesn't mean it has to be formal.

When a young couple with three children bought a new Georgian-style house in one of Atlanta's most gracious neighborhoods, they asked me to come take a look. I could see what had attracted them—the architecture was magnificent. Their new home had the scale and proportions of a grand old English country house. But there was one problem. All the moldings and pediments and cornices were very formal, but the family was not.

Nobody wanted to tamper with the existing architecture, but I decided to soften it a bit. In the entrance hall, the details had been picked out in various colors, which made it seem very dressy. The room became simpler and purer after we painted the walls, the trim, and the ceiling bone white. Then I waxed the walls to add a little patina. On either side of the hall was a large doorway. One led to the dining room, the other to the library. Each doorway was topped by a pediment and framed in pilasters, and I thought it would be interesting to paint just that woodwork a subtle gray-

This entrance hall has it all—great architecture and extraordinary details. The woodwork around the side door is painted a pale gray-green, but the rest is bone white. The white simplifies a space that could have felt very imposing. The French antique wing chair helps bring it down to human scale as well, and a Russian mahogany table provides a central focal point.

green. That way, I made sure you noticed the detail, but the rest of the room remained pure white. Now the doorways almost seem as if they are in shadow, which adds another layer of softness to the space.

One of the things I like best about classical architecture is the way one room opens onto another, without a hallway in between. I like being able to stand in one room and see into the next, and I'll often use color to lead you from one to the other. In this case, I took the gray-green from the doorways and used it in a slightly darker version on the woodwork in the dining room. Then I had a de Gournay wall-paper custom-colored in the same gray-greens. I love those hand-painted, scenic wallpapers. They're the epitome of classic elegance to me. In a new house, they're a designer's silver bullet because they create instant patina. And since you can custom-color them, it gives me a chance to pull all the colors of a house into one room in a subtle way. I don't use wall coverings very often. I happen to prefer the clarity of paint. But for de Gournay or Gracie hand-painted

I love dressmaker details like the ribbon ties and corded trim on the linen slipcovers, which are also monogrammed. In a room as elegant as this, you might expect an Oriental rug, but we went with more casual sisal. The hand-painted wallpaper by de Gournay portrays a hunting scene. The paint on the trim is Ralph Lauren's Throne.

wallpapers, I will make an exception. Like any good investment, they just get better and better over time.

The same thing is true of fine antiques. A good piece will hold its value, and you will treasure it forever. My attitude has always been to buy less, if you have to, but buy the best. You can't go wrong with a Chippendale chair. In this dining room, we slipcovered the Chippendale chairs in natural linen. Then I took the same linen and made it into curtains, with an elegant tassel trim along the leading edge. Now there's a lovely play in the room between formality and informality. You still have the fine carved wood and the antique porcelain, but suddenly, with the slipcovers, it feels friendlier to me. I like to give people options. There is more than one way to live in this space.

I follow the same process in every house. First, I study the architecture and make any adjustments that are needed. Once you get the architecture right, you can take the decorating in any direction. You can dress a house up or down, fill it with antiques or contemporary furniture. Just choose each piece carefully. Don't let anything into your rooms unless it has meaning for you. Then your home will always give you great pleasure. It will be an instant classic.

What a spectacular entryway, with that beautifully curved staircase and the black-and-white marble floor. Architecturally, there was enough going on without highlighting the moldings in another color of paint. When walls and moldings are the same color, I think you appreciate the dimensionality in another way. It becomes very sculptural.

FOLLOWING PAGE: Probably the most beautiful chandelier I have ever found is in this dining room. It's French from the 1920s, gilt bronze and crystal, and reminds me of a crown. The de Gournay wallpaper is hand-painted in the most muted tones so the pattern is subtle. I had skirts made for the English Chippendale-style chairs, which makes them a little less formal. In a room this large, it's nice to be able to work in a little more fabric to soften the space. The sisal rug also tones down the formality.

You can see back into the living room from the family dining room, and I picked up the taupe color on the door surrounds and the cornice. Then I had the walls painted and waxed in a golden ochre, a deeper version of the tones in the living room. I like to build up a sequence of color from room to room. The dining chairs are covered in a classic Bennison print, which I also used for the curtains.

RIGHT: Almost everything in this living room is bone or taupe or cream, and then we pulled a pale rose out of the Oushak rug and did a rose silk flange on the taupe slipcovers and a taupe welting on the sofa. That's the way I often do color—just a touch. The nineteenth-century *trumeau* on the mantel echoes a blue-gray found in the rug. The pale blue of the porcelain collection is picked up in the lamp shades.

I love moody colors, the kind that often have an undertone of gray. They have the aura of an older world. They're quiet, mysterious, peaceful.

The dining chairs are the most beautiful blue-gray, and when we found that antique buffet cabinet in the same blue-gray, I knew it belonged in this room. A vintage wallpaper panel hangs above it.

RIGHT: The walls are papered in a pale celadon-green shagreen, which is like a suggestion of stone. Even when the room is in shadow, there's always a gleam of light from the antique crystal chandelier or the gilded mirror or the crystal candlesticks on the French limestone fireplace. The Greek key border on the curtains is another classical note.

A dining room can usually handle more color and pattern than any other room in the house. You're only in it for small periods of time. Why not make it memorable?

The turquoise grass cloth on the walls and the vaguely retro pattern on the curtains and that drop-dead mirror give this dining room a kind of 1940s Moderne look. I was thrilled when we found those curlicue chairs—they're like the long-lost cousin to that mirror—but there were only three. So I did what I often do and mixed in another style, a chalky white-painted wood chair with a classic oval back. I have no problem with putting dark and light woods together.

RIGHT: The curlicue chair has a turquoise mohair seat and the oval-backed chair is upholstered in bone-white leather, outlined with nail heads on a turquoise grosgrain ribbon. The rug picks up a hint of turquoise in its pattern. The perfect finishing touch is that vase—the deepest of all these blues.

This is a very American version of an English country house, with the dining room wide open to the living room. It's a more relaxed, casual way of living.

The warm orange on the walls—Farrow & Ball's Orangery—seems to come right out of the Oushak rug, and then I had the paint waxed to create a leatherlike effect. Fine antique furniture, like the Sheraton buffet, makes it feel as if the family has lived here forever. The fabrics all share a similar tone, so the two rooms blend into each other.

Riding boots, walking sticks, an old French tapestry—these are the kinds of objects that create mood. They start to tell a story as soon as you walk in the door.

This entrance hall is an odd shape—a long rectangle—and I needed something to pull it together. I had a custom wall covering made in a damask pattern by Walter Knabe and used it to cover the ceiling. It's unexpected and subtle, and I like the juxtaposition with the board on the walls. A collection of antique maps is hung in a grid, which creates a strong architectural element to anchor that wall.

RIGHT: The warm honey tones and the intriguing shapes make this composition very pleasing. I love the contrast of clear glass against the dense colors and textures of the tapestry. The blossoming branches have a wonderfully wild shape. I'll often use them in place of flowers. They're less fussy.

I like to
layer texture
and color
to make a
room look
richer.

The hallway leading to the bedroom had plenty of room
and a beautiful view, so I put an antique French desk by the
window. That old Italian chair is an amazing piece—look at
those cone-shaped legs.

RIGHT: The bedroom is all caramel and bone, and the colors
began with the graphic Kelly Wearstler linen that I used
to upholster the walls. It makes the room feel cozy, in a
contemporary way. All the various textures layered in the
same tones add more warmth and softness. There's a silk on
the headboard, linen velvet on the chair, Fortuny cotton on the
pillow, a cashmere throw on the bench, and sisal on the floor.

I used a mix
of antiques
that felt
timeless, yet
fresh enough
for a growing
family.

This Biedermeier secretary is one of my most favorite pieces. It's so strong architecturally that it anchors the room.

LEFT: There is something so magical about an antique Coromandel screen. It adds patina, depth, and scale and immediately grounds a room. I like the juxtaposition of the high-backed contemporary sofa and the nineteenth-century landscape painting. Two stools are more unexpected than the typical coffee table, and more versatile. All the walls, trim, and ceiling are painted in Benjamin Moore's Elephant Tusk.

I have always loved Biedermeier furniture. It has the most beautiful lines and strong, graphic detailing.

Inspired by an antique Biedermeier sofa and secretary, we took the burl wood and black inlays and re-created them on the walls and mantel of this library.

RIGHT: This client is a true collector and has acquired many Biedermeier pieces, like the pedestal table, which are all showcased in this room. A Regency chair stands by the fireplace, near a wrought-iron easel. Books share space on the shelves with her collection of miniature rooms. The floor is lacquered black to match the inlay.

This hallway off the living room was so large that we had enough space to create a freestanding, oval wooden bar in the center of it. The little gold-painted medallions are an architectural detail that we used as a motif.

RIGHT: There is nothing quite like an Oriental rug in a paneled room. The red leather ottoman builds on the warmth of the wood. I decided to do a one-cushion sofa, which is a more modern note in a very traditional room.

Sophisticated Simplicity

I LIKE ROOMS THAT HAVE A KIND OF INTEGRITY. Everything in them seems to belong. There is nothing extraneous. When I walk into a room, I want it to feel clear and clean. Always, at the back of my head, I hear the words "Less is more." It's absolutely true. One great object can have more impact than four.

You have to know how to edit if you want to build a beautiful room. It's a hard thing to do, especially when it comes to your own favorite possessions. Sometimes you have to bring in someone with an unprejudiced eye to help you decide what to keep, and what to put away. The idea is to be disciplined. I will keep rearranging and refining the objects in a room until I get the mix just right—old and new, dark and light, smooth and rough, straight and curved. There's something eye-catching about contrast, as well as continuity. When I look at my work, I notice that I'm always pulling similar objects together, rather than putting one drawing here and one there, for example. If you hang all your drawings in a group,

Displaying objects is an art. You can have multiple things and still create order. I've grouped the pictures on the wall into a composition. The shape of the frames is echoed in the leather inserts on the chest. Even the leather-bound books on the shelves are arranged architecturally, almost like building blocks, to create a pleasing pattern.

they will have more impact. And you can actually get more of them up on the wall, while still keeping the effect very strong and simple. It's the perfect solution for a collector, like me, who still wants a room to have a clean look.

I can't think if I'm surrounded by clutter. I need a certain amount of order in my space. One way to organize things is to repeat colors and shapes. In an entrance hall, I might hang two pictures, both the same size and framed the same way, to flank a central doorway. A pair of chairs marks the entrance to the living room and sets up a pleasing symmetry. Instinctively, most people like things to feel balanced. Repetition is also very calming. But if you have too many bits and pieces around a room, the eye can't take them all in and it becomes confusing. You don't know where to look first.

It's not my style to overdecorate. I don't like all the frills. I don't want all the fuss. I'm not fond of fancy swags and ruffles. What's the point of doing a window treatment that's so elaborate it overwhelms the window? I don't want to cut off the light, and I like to see the view. The most you're going to get on one of my curtains is a contrasting color as a trim, or a tassel along an edge. I prefer a simple, tailored look. Or even no curtains at all. I want you to see the beautiful arch at the top of those French doors. Some people may think a long, low chaise is an unusual piece to put in

The contrast of dark wood and light walls animates this entrance hall. The limestone floor has its own pattern of dark and light, and that graphic quality is accentuated by the zebra rug. I'm always attracted to armillary spheres, like the one on the table. Somehow, with that bold shape, they're both classic and modern at the same time.

an entrance hall, but it actually works. You can drop your coat and bag on it as you come in. I like the softness of the upholstery against the stone floor. And if you put a table next to it, you feel as if you might actually sit down there with a drink. All you need is one great piece of furniture, like a chaise, to give a whole new character to a space. I'm not interested in a piece unless it has personality. And if I can't find what I want, I don't believe in buying something just to fill up a room. When people are redecorating a house, they often think they have to do everything at once. But I always tell my clients, "Don't rush." If you're willing to wait, the right piece will eventually appear.

This entrance hall, with rotundas at each end, is an interesting blend of classical and modern architecture. You might expect to see two consoles as you walk in, but instead we built cantilevered ledges that float. They seem like an extension of the architecture. Above them, I hung two lithographs by Joan Miró. The walls of the rotunda in the background are covered in pale green silk. The sculpture is by Michael Lucerno.

This is a spectacular space architecturally, with a contemporary version of a classic Palladian window that is almost 20 feet high. Anything I put in front of it needed to have a similar scale and sense of drama. I was delighted to find that mahogany Empire-style library table with touches of gilt on the legs. A collection of pottery, in different shapes but with the same blue glaze, is grouped for more impact. I like the symmetry of the two Swedish Biedermeier chairs, and the two Franz Kline collages, which flank the window and seem to frame the table as well.

RIGHT: There's a trick to hanging art, and the secret is to keep it low. Most people would have left a lot more white space between the sofa and the painting, but I think it's more powerful this way. The colors in the pillows seem to bleed straight into the painting, which was done by Joe Richardson.

I like to do the
background in
one neutral color,
which unifies
the shell and
strengthens the
architecture. It
also shows off
the furniture so
beautifully.

This living room is huge—20 by 40 feet—and there's a
stunning clarity to the volume, since it also has a 20-
foot ceiling. The last thing I wanted to do was clutter
it up. So I tried something a little different. I set two
sofas right against the long wall so you look out
over the full width of the room to the windows. That
way, you really appreciate the sense of space. And
then I livened up each seating area with the most
extraordinary chairs. The Empire-style library table
acts as a link between the two sides of the room.

A doorway frames a view from one room to another, and I think you should always put something in the frame. Here, in a hallway, I made a vignette composed of a modern cabinet, two iron sconces, a plaster deer head, and a collection of 1950s Italian and Swedish glass. What do any of these things have to do with each other? Well, they all have very strong lines and intriguing shapes. I like the juxtaposition of squares and curves, dark and light—and then that burst of gorgeous color.

RIGHT: A trestle table in the entryway can be set for dining—which makes more sense than a dedicated dining room in a beach house like this (see the table as it normally looks on page 135). The bench alongside it is less formal than chairs, more versatile, and can be pushed underneath when not in use. The walls and floors are painted white, but it's the blue accents—the stripe on the chairs, the leafy cut-velvet on the bench, and the crisp border on the curtains—that carry the room.

The dining room opens to a rotunda, where the walls are lined in yellow silk. It's a brilliant flash of color, and I did the cool-blue paint in the dining room as a contrast. The colors are so strong and the architecture is so pure that you really don't need much else. I chose the Regency-style table for its clean lines. The chairs, in dark brown leather and painted wood, are so graphic they become almost sculptural. Andy Warhol's *Judy Garland* has a similar play of dark and light.

In order to get a room right, I'll often subtract rather than add. Of course, what's left has to be very good in order to sustain the attention.

It's hard to compete with a chair shaped like a baseball glove, so I found a spot in the sunroom where I could feature it. An image of James Dean by Russell Young hangs nearby.

RIGHT: Two sculptures on balsa wood by Jean Dubuffet hang above a cabinet by Barbara Barry. I love the contrast in color and shape. Each piece in this corner, from the Rose Tarlow chair to the three-legged lamp, has great lines and a strong personality. Their styles are completely different. It's only their strength—and that touch of gold leaf on the furniture—that holds them together.

If you get the
background right,
you don't have to
overdo what you
put into it.

This bedroom is painted a lovely Limoges blue—Westerly
Wind by Glidden—which sets a cool, restful mood, and I
picked up the color in the bed linens and the lamps. The
four-poster bed is so unusual that you really don't need
much else. I added the mirrored nightstand, which feels so
light and airy, for a note of glamour.

RIGHT: The Gustavian desk is antique and the club chair is
comfortably old-fashioned, but the wall of cabinets is purely
contemporary. It has clean, clear lines and my signature
X-motif, yet it doesn't overwhelm the room. It blends right
in and offers an extraordinary amount of storage. Hidden
behind it are the closet and the TV.

Champagne pink and chocolate brown, combined so strikingly in the curtains, make a great palette for a master bedroom because it manages to be both feminine and masculine at the same time. Here, the feminine comes to the fore with the custom mirrored headboard and the pink satin-covered antique chair. Then the campaign desk at the foot of the bed has a more masculine quality and seems to balance it out.

RIGHT: The contemporary sofa is really deep—which means it's easy to curl up in—and is covered with the same warm brown velvet that is on the curtains. The armchairs are new, but that white trellis pattern gives them a stylized 1930s look. The whole room captures a kind of Hollywood glamour.

You can have all the traditional comforts, but done in a slightly different way so the room feels fresh and new.

This is not your typical vanity. The water runs into freestanding bowls instead of the usual undermounted sink, and the countertop is made from poured concrete—5 inches thick, for more impact. No cupboard doors, just an open shelf underneath to hold stacks of towels. The mosaic tiles behind the mirrors have a golden shimmer.

RIGHT: Here's how scale can really work for you. Imagine that mirror on the wall in a more normal size. It just wouldn't look as good, would it? In this huge size, it's like an enormous jewel, and it sets a very romantic tone. The tub, supported on dark wooden legs, is distinctive. It's an old style done in a new way. I like the silvery look of the little pedestal table, made of metal. Everything here, including the mosaic tiles on the wall, has a watery sheen.

Luxurious Ease

PEOPLE THINK OF COMFORT AND BEAUTY as two separate things, but they're actually indivisible for me. If I walk into a room and there's no inviting place to sit, I'm not going to stay there very long. It doesn't matter how pretty the room is. If a room is really inviting, people will use it, and rooms that are lived in become more and more beautiful to me.

A fireplace is a definite draw. I often start there and bring the furniture up close and arrange it into a conversational group. Even in a very large room, I try to create a sense of intimacy. In a study, I might choose the same fabric for all the chairs. In a living room, I might choose colors and textures that are all variations on the same tone to create a sense of agreement, even if the pieces have different personalities. Color and pattern and shape are important because we also perceive comfort visually.

Think about something as basic as the chairs around a dining table. A traditional dining chair with a carved, wooden back does not look as tempting as a chair with a little more upholstery. That is where I would want

Instead of the usual sofa and two chairs, I arranged four chairs in a circle in front of the fireplace in this library. It's more intimate this way, and great for conversation. Those chairs, in a luxurious cognac-colored linen velvet, just say comfort to me. The rug picks up the same tone. The bookcases and the walls are painted in a pale gray so they blend into one other, but the wood on the mantel is just stained and waxed. It needs to be strong to stand up to the mirror, which is slightly overscale.

FOLLOWING PAGE: In a Normandy-style house, those antique French chairs by the fireplace set the mood, but I've also mixed in more contemporary pieces like the armless sofa and the iron coffee table. I love that quirky, low-slung Swedish chair on the left. A chest of drawers is probably not what you would expect to see in that niche, but it fits. The mix gives you a sense of ease and freedom. The painting above the mantel is by Dusty Griffith.

to sit, if we're going to linger over dinner. I help my clients think about how they're going to live in the house, in order to decide what each room needs. If you're building a new house, it makes very good sense to get an interior designer involved from the very beginning. While the architect is dealing with structural issues of form and mass, I'm thinking about a mudroom, walk-in closets, French doors, a breakfast room, and a larger pantry by the kitchen. These are the kind of details that affect your quality of life. If we get them right, you will feel happier in the house.

Once the architectural questions are resolved, I can focus on each individual room. When I'm designing, I'm thinking about how people will move through a space and what furniture they will need. I'm working out how to layer color and pattern and texture, as well as form. I want to appeal to all the senses. Certain fabrics look so soft, you just have to touch them. I want to provide places where the eye can stop and rest, as well as places to sit comfortably. The room should flow smoothly, visually as well as physically.

I want the design to pull you into the space, and make you feel like you never want to leave. In order to create that effect, I need to know what kind of chair you like and how you react to certain colors. I want to know what you love, and what makes you feel special. Then I try to translate all of those opinions and emotions into fabrics and furniture and accessories. I want to make a house that relates specifically to you, and then you will feel completely at home in it.

When chairs in a dining room are all the same, it becomes very stiff, like a conference room. I try to break it up. Notice how the woods don't match. The tall, upholstered chairs are done in the same fabric as the curtains. It's nice to see the pattern all spread out. I hung lanterns by the fireplace because they cast a lovely glow, and put all the lights on a dimmer. The walls are painted in Antique Sterling by Glidden.

If you want to pack more people into a tight space, your best choice is a sectional sofa. The L-shape creates a very strong line and utilizes every square inch, even the corner.

This is a found space on a second-floor landing overlooking a two-story living room. I thought, why not furnish it? I didn't have a lot of square footage to work with, which is why I chose a sectional sofa. The ottoman doubles as more casual seating or a coffee table. Both pieces are covered in natural linen—one solid and the other in a geometric print. A few accent pillows pick up the blues. I found that licorice-colored leather chair and thought it would give this spot a whole other level of sophistication. It's a dark note that echoes the window mullions and the ottoman's legs and somehow pulls the whole area together.

The limestone on the kitchen floor continues right through the family room and then out onto the terrace, to connect indoors and outdoors.

With all the limestone on this terrace, you almost feel as if you're in the south of France. The arrangement of furniture, with a virtual path down the middle, seems to draw you out even farther toward the limestone fountain.

RIGHT: This kitchen, with a magnificent limestone chimneypiece over the stove, seems to have been transported straight from a French château. The refrigerator and other appliances are hidden behind cabinetry that looks more like furniture than built-ins. A zinc-topped table with an iron base is surrounded by old cracked-leather chairs, which add a wonderful patina.

An antique trestle table in the entryway feels very welcoming, with two large ottomans where you could conceivably sit, or put down a bag. It's a nice way to get you to come in and stop and get a feel for the space before moving on.

RIGHT: The high-backed sofas bring a huge room down to a more human scale and establish an intimate space for conversation. The linen upholstery and the sisal rug feel very casual. It's always a challenge to find something new to do with a mantel. This time, I kept it strong and simple with a graphic sunburst mirror and just two gilded Italian reliquaries. At first you might think they're too ornate for this room, but I like the contrast they set up with the old, rough-hewn beams, and they have the right scale.

Those rustic beams were salvaged from a 200-year-old Georgia barn, and they lift the eye right up to the ceiling, which, like the walls, is painted in Benjamin Moore's Floral White. This is a very large room, so I divided it into two main seating areas. The wall of French doors could have looked very cold, but I warmed it up with those burnt-orange curtains. They are hung very simply from rings on an iron pole, and just puddle on the floor. I did not want them to look overdone. When you don't have all those flounces and tiebacks, the curtains hang straight and you can actually see the intricacies of the pattern. I spend a lot of time choosing my fabrics, and I like to feature them.

When you do
something very
simple, like an
all-white room,
you have to have
enough detail so
it looks finished.

The dark wood floors make the cabinetry in this kitchen look
even whiter. It's very cool and clean, with granite countertops
and stainless-steel appliances. Even the dishes on display are
consistently dark brown or white.

RIGHT: The furniture in the breakfast area is covered in simple
Belgian linen, but there are various details that make it special.
The slipcovers on the chairs are finished with a dark brown
flange, and the linen curtains are trimmed in whimsical wooden
tassels. The bench is unexpected, and more casual than two
more chairs. I love the hanging light fixture by Thomas O'Brien,
because it looks simultaneously vintage and modern.

As soon as I had bookcases built into all four corners of this room, it seemed to pull together. The old leather-bound books add patina and texture, and then I layered in more texture with fabrics like linen and linen velvet (on that delightfully roomy ottoman) and a creamy Oushak rug. The palette is cream and caramel, with a little bit of blue thrown in. The room would be a lot less interesting without those two blue chairs. That one touch of bright, contrasting color is a small surprise that makes the room feel even more personal and unique.

I put this lovely, architectural Swedish bench in the hallway so you're not looking at a blank wall when you're sitting at the dining table. The tapestry is just the right scale to hang above it, and it has a muted tone-on-tone quality. It adds incredible warmth and texture. I love to buy old tapestries when I can find them. They also add a sense of history and always look good behind a console table or a bed.

RIGHT: This is a big wall, so I've broken it into sections by hanging different groupings of art. On the left, I stacked three antique prints and then did a looser composition of sunburst mirrors—some old, some new—over the sofa. They're very randomly hung, which adds to their charm.

You don't expect to see such formal Louis XV-style dining chairs in a kitchen, but they actually look great around the old French farm table, which warms them up a bit so they don't feel quite so fancy. It looks as if you're putting family heirlooms to good use.

This family loves to eat in the kitchen, and they wanted it to feel like a classic European house. They definitely did not want the usual granite-topped island. Instead, we were after an old-world look, with glass-fronted cabinets and a farmhouse sink. But I did mix messages a bit. That's an industrial-size faucet, with sprayer, and the light fixture is a modern version of a traditional chandelier.

PART III

ELEMENTS

Architectural Elements

I THINK IN THREE DIMENSIONS. When clients are building a new house, I always walk them through the floor plan first to make sure everyone understands the flow of the rooms and their relative size. I pay attention to proportions—the height of a ceiling, the width of a door. A good architect creates strong volumes. Even empty, a room can be beautiful if it has a beautifully designed shell.

Often, I will take my cues from the architecture. In a clean, contemporary space, I may subtract rather than add furnishings. All you need is one or two good pieces, with enough breathing room around them to show off their lines. Restraint can be very powerful. There is nothing quite so exciting to me as pure white walls.

The architecture establishes a certain order, and I have to work within it. If it's good, I will make sure the furniture doesn't get in the way. If the furniture has to carry the room, it better be able to sustain the attention. I've been lucky enough to work with very talented architects over the course of my career. Their work has inspired me.

A dramatic staircase like this is a great gift. The ceiling in this entrance hall is two stories high, and all that was there to begin with was that central medallion. The rest of the motif is trompe l'oeil. Those aren't real coffers, just paint. We expanded on the detail to create a more powerful effect.

When you paint a room all white, you lose any sense of boundaries. Suddenly the space seems infinitely big.

Light streams through the fanlight and the sidelights around the front door, and the whole room seems to glisten. Everything in the entrance hall—walls, trim, ceiling, and door—is painted in Bone China by Sherwin-Williams. Somehow the touches of blue on the Swedish neoclassical side chairs from Versace's estate and the vase make the white paint feel even fresher. The gilt has a luminous quality, too, and makes the chairs and the console look almost ready to levitate. Imagine how different the effect would be if the furnishings were made of mahogany.

FOLLOWING PAGE: Good architecture embodies memory. A stately entrance hall like this, with marble floors and classical columns, takes you back to another period in history. It gives the room a fourth dimension—time. There's really no need to do a lot of decorating when the bones of a room are this good. I painted the walls in one of my favorite blues—Glidden's Sevres Blue—which gives them more of a presence. The blue also shows off the white marble fountain, in contrast. The doors are painted black. The columns are actually wood, painted to look like stone. The architecture is so powerful that there is really no need for furniture.

I painted all
the woodwork
a beautiful
shade of bone.
When the color
is consistent, I
think it's easier
to focus on the
minute details
of the carving.

Everything is bone except the inside of the bookcases,
which I did in a dark taupe-gray to accentuate the
arches and add more depth. I filled the shelves with
books instead of the usual plates, to make the room
also work as a library. Then I had the high-backed
banquettes specially made for each corner. They
add a contemporary note to a traditional room, while
offering another place to sit. I like the feeling that you
could just pull any one of the upholstered chairs up
to the table. A large hanging lamp with a shade feels
more modern than a standard chandelier.

I like to build
bookshelves
into a bedroom.
Books add
another layer
of personality.
Besides, I love
to read in bed.
Of course, it's
also nice to have
a comfortable
chair and a big
library table.

The two chairs flanking this Empire-style library table
are French antiques, upholstered in camel-colored
linen velvet. The linen curtains and the felt rug are in
similar shades. I like to use a single color in layer after
layer to add richness. Don't miss the doors—another
opportunity for architecture. They're exceptionally
tall, with great hardware and distinctive panels.

I love that
X-motif.
It has delicacy
and strength.

In a wrought-iron railing, the X looks very striking and contemporary. I added another element, the crosspieces in the center, which almost turn it into a star.

OPPOSITE: The X-shaped cross bracing is actually an old Roman motif, so it brings a sense of history to these bookcases. A diagonal always energizes space and animates a room. And I'll tell you a little secret: Whenever you do a bookcase like this with glass doors, it doesn't really matter if the books are perfectly arranged on the shelves. The Xs create an impression of order.

Everybody loves a classic white kitchen with glass-fronted cabinets, but doesn't it look even better when the mullions are in the shape of an X? The X motif can look formal or informal, sophisticated or country, depending on the context. Here, the cabinetry is charmingly old-fashioned. I like to put a kitchen sink by a window, if possible, because it's nice to look at a view.

OPPOSITE: The challenge with a range is, how do you hide the vent? We built a chimneypiece that masks the hood and gives you that fireplace effect, as if you were still cooking on the hearth. The backsplash behind the range is done in the same granite as the countertops and recessed to form a convenient shelf for oils and other seasonings used every day.

Objects and Details

I'M A COLLECTOR. I find things I love and I buy them, not always knowing exactly what I'm going to do with them. I just keep acquiring more beautiful things. Their attraction, for me, has nothing to do with price. I can go into a junk shop and unearth something interesting, and it will mean just as much to me as the finest antique. If I like a piece, I'm not really worried about where it came from or what century it was made. I'm searching for style and personality. Sometimes you find it in the strangest places.

For years, I have to admit that I could never leave Paris without picking up another little Eiffel Tower. I've got dozens, made of metal, wire, crystal, paper, silver, and porcelain. And even now, if I'm rushing through the airport and one catches my eye, I can't resist. When I'm doing a house with clients, I'm always trying to get them to think about that last layer, all those funny little things that mean something to them and will stamp the room

All of my pieces for Hickory Chair have very distinct personalities, yet somehow they all go together. My Antoinette side table with mirrored sides and top was inspired by a table I found at the Paris flea market. The Frederica bench is upholstered in an overscale stripe I made myself, out of two different fabrics. I'll use that effect when I want to create more impact. I'm particularly fond of the hand-carved Alexandra chair with the quatrefoil back, which I named after my daughter. The prints with intaglios and seashells are from my Soicher-Marin collection. The Trianon table lamps are from my collection for Visual Comfort.

FOLLOWING PAGE: If I had to pinpoint what all these pieces from my collection have in common, I would say that they have great lines and very interesting shapes. You can definitely see the French influence, especially when they're all upholstered in plain white muslin.

with their personality. I don't think a room is done until you have found those accessories. Objects carry emotions. There is something about a cracked-leather club chair or a finely carved four-poster bed that feels comfortable and familiar. They can give a new room a sense of history. And if a space needs personality, one of the quickest ways to add it is with an unusual piece of furniture. All you need is one interesting chair to liven up a seating group. I can also be tempted by the sheen of dark wood or a chalky painted finish. It's getting harder and harder to find the kinds of pieces I like, and now I have the opportunity to design my own. My collections for Hickory Chair, Lee Jofa, Visual Comfort, Soicher-Marin, and Safavieh are the culmination of years spent studying interior design. I took some of my favorite antiques and did my own interpretations. The original French piece that inspired the Frederica bench has been sitting at my dining table for years. I was so happy to be able to do the kind of detailing I adore, like nail-head trim along a grosgrain ribbon. I've used the quatrefoil—such a classic architectural detail that is seen in old buildings, fashion, and jewelry—in my Alexandra chair, with its hand-carved back. These are the kinds of pieces that set a tone and create a mood. They are stylish and personal and timeless.

There's something about the combination of a mirror over a console table that is practically foolproof. It always works, even if the two pieces aren't from the same period. In this case, the tall, slim proportions of the mirror seem to continue the lines of the gilt-wood table. Then the drawing, propped off-center, makes the arrangement a little more casual. The whole composition becomes even more inviting when you bring in an antique leather chair like this, one of my prized finds from the Paris flea market.

Proportion is
everything.
When you get
it right, the whole
room soars.

ABOVE: I like the exceptionally tall, slim back of this
French chair, which gives it a period look. And then
I dressed it in a slipcover skirt with inverted pleats.
Fashion has always been a big influence on me. I'll
take a detail from the couture shows and translate
it into upholstery.

RIGHT: I collect Eiffel Towers, in any form. Here's
one on an old postcard, and another in a locket.

OPPOSITE: Take a small object and frame it with a
large mat and you have instant drama. There's also
something interesting about the way I hung the
frames—two by two, straight up from the table—in
an unusually tall stack. The composition itself
becomes almost architectural. The bronze figures
on the table are by Tom Corbin.

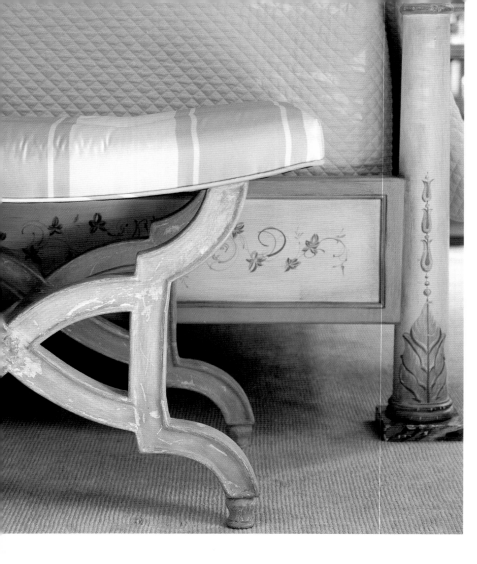

I don't want
a room to
look decorated.
It should
look collected.

ABOVE: The hand-painted detail on this bed is so beautifully done, right down to the leaves on its foot. A piece like this becomes an instant heirloom.

RIGHT: A fine antique, like this eighteenth-century Italian chair, will hold its value. The old damask upholstery was so pretty that I left it exactly how we found it. The curtains in back are made of silk and trimmed in velvet patterned with a Greek key.

OPPOSITE: The decorative painting on the chest softens it and gives the eye something to linger on. Each piece in this room feels carefully chosen and very special, like that starburst mirror. The antique chair is upholstered in a soft blue that echoes the curtains and the walls.

You need more on a
bookshelf than
just books. I like
to break it up with
objects and pictures
that show off my
client's personality.

I'll often hang pictures right on a bookcase. I like that layered look.
The Asheworth campaign desk, with X-shaped legs, and the Hunt
chairs are part of my Hickory Chair collection.

OPPOSITE: Bookcases on wheels—very convenient. These are my
Prado bookcases for Hickory Chair, and each is made of two units
that can be stacked, as they are here, or used separately. The
wood shelves are easily adjustable, and I managed to incorporate
my X-motif into the back. I like the fact that they look industrial
and modern and traditional, all at the same time.

Dressmaker details make my upholstery very special.

The tassels run along the edge of a curtain to add texture and a little playfulness. I'll use tape to outline the shape of a sofa cushion, or take one fabric and turn it in two different directions on the same piece. When I'm making a slipcover, I like to trim the edges with a flat flange or a contrasting cord to introduce a color from another part of the room into the upholstery. It's a small surprise that really uplifts the piece.

RIGHT: Nail heads add rhythm, order, and definition, and give my Candler bed a handcrafted look.

Color and Light

PEOPLE ALWAYS SPEAK OF MY WORK and color in the same breath. But if you look at the houses I've done, you'll see that there are actually very few rooms painted a solid bright red or yellow or green. That's not the way I typically work. Instead, I use color very strategically. It might appear on just one wall, or in a fabric on a chair, or in the accessories. Oddly enough, I think it has even more impact that way.

I use color to make people feel good. Color can lift your mood. Color conveys personality. I talk to clients and look closely at what they wear in order to figure out the colors they like. Blue has always been one of the most mesmerizing colors for me. I'm attracted to almost any shade of blue, all the way from that moody French gray-blue to Limoges blue to turquoise and aqua and that deep, watery blue-green. I like colors with depth. Whenever I go to Europe, I fall in love all over again with that European sensibility. There, every color seems to contain many other hues, maybe because it has been painted over so many times. I love those rich, indescribable shades.

If you're going to use a bright color like peony pink—Checkberry from Glidden—make sure it has depth. For me, that means you can see many different shades in it—red and pink and ochre and white. Color is made up of other colors, and sometimes I'll pull out one of those secondary shades and use it elsewhere in the room. The raffia upholstery has that same ochre tone. All these colors carry light and make this dining room feel warm and inviting.

The colors feel muted and subtle—and then you notice that one wall is painted a very intense pink. That's the way I like to use color—as an accent that elevates the whole room. Something that could have been ordinary suddenly becomes sublime.

When we were painting that one wall, everyone was shocked because it was so pink. But once we got everything else into the room, it all balanced out. The pink seems to be plucked from one of the flowers on that painted panel. Then there are all sorts of golden tones on the furniture and the sconces. A few flourishes hold the room together—the extravagantly curved table legs relate to the equally exuberant curves on the consoles and the chandelier.

But I also gravitate to clear colors, the ones that seem to embody light. When I'm designing a room, I start from light. I analyze the light in a room before I do anything. What direction is the light coming from? Is it soft or harsh? Light is intrinsically connected to color for me. The choice of color depends on the light. You should never pick a paint color without brushing on a sample first and seeing how it looks in your room. The exact same color will look very different in different types of light. And a good quality paint, with lots of pigment, will change color over the course of a day, which makes it seem more vibrant and alive.

Often, the light in a room leads me to shades of white. White is my basic building block. And then as you go through the rooms in a house, the colors may unfold into deeper tones of ivory and cream and taupe. Adding color to a house is a layering process for me. I've noticed that it's easier to add more colors when they all have the same value. Then they're roughly the same depth, in terms of lightness and darkness. That creates an easy sequence through the rooms. The transition isn't jarring; it's smooth. The colors feel almost integral to the house. You can't even imagine it without them.

The floors and the fireplace wall in this beach house are finished in a cool, clean white, and then I played with various shades of blue. The walls in the sitting room beyond are a sky blue; the slipcover on the chair is more of a French blue. The rug is striped in other blues. The various textures—including the iridescent blown-glass balls—add to the story. There's a watery feeling, enhanced by the convex mirrors, which remind me of portholes. The painting is by Dusty Griffith.

Sometimes a
random object
can drive
the whole
color palette
in a room.

I found the deep turquoise-blue lamps and then I
pulled in other blue tones, from the pale blue on the
sofa pillows to the murkier blue and brown on the
chair. The mottled mirror on the cabinet reflects
the light and adds a silvery sheen. The paint on the
walls is Rain by Sherwin-Williams.

My method
is simple. I
strategically
layer color to
build up the
effect in a room.

White walls and floors set off the deliberate touches of blue in this entryway
that also doubles as a dining area. There's really only one object—the seashell
chandelier— that says *beach*. Too many beach-related items can get too theme-y.

RIGHT: The upholstery on the bench, the chairs, and collection of vintage
glass—that's all the blue. But isn't it interesting how the whole room feels blue?

FOLLOWING PAGE: We painted this dining room in three coats of Glidden's Seven
Lakes—an intoxicatingly deep turquoise blue. You really feel as if you are
swimming in color. I added a sea green on the curtain flange and the fabric on the
back of the Jansen chairs; the front is in turquoise linen velvet. The table is by
Jansen as well, and then we mixed in those whimsical white-painted chairs just
to shake it up a bit. Painting the walls and the trim all the same color looks very
contemporary, but it's actually a traditional eighteenth-century technique.

When putting a room together, I'll often choose accessories that in some way bring out the beauty of the art.

The vibrant oranges in the painting by Andrew Saftel seem to spin off into the fabric on the chair and the flowers in the vase.

LEFT: I like mixing periods, and would never hesitate to put a contemporary painting over an antique console. I picked up the touches of gold in the painting with the bowl and the balls and the berries.

The repetition of the raspberry color
pulls together a lot of very different
furniture styles in this room. The
antique French chairs have a whole
new relationship to the French
Moderne stools when they're done
in the same raspberry and white.
And then I pulled the color onto
the platinum linen-velvet sofa with
a Greek key-patterned raspberry
tape that outlines the cushions
and trims the skirt. The artwork,
unconventionally made of nail polish
on paper, is by Scott Ingram.

I love beautiful
fabrics. I'll
often save the
boldest pattern
for the curtains,
and hang them
floor to ceiling.
They can have
such an impact
on a room.

In this sunroom, I wanted a timeworn look. There's a gray, weathered glaze on the walls. The curtains, made from a Scalamandre fabric, are reminiscent of the past. The cane chair is English and the birdcage is French; both date from the late 1800s. A mosaic insert on the limestone floor picks up all the colors in the curtains and adds another little eccentricity.

RIGHT: I couldn't resist those enormous roses. That's actually the only pink in an otherwise neutral room. The pattern was also the right scale for those exceptionally tall, arched windows.

Color makes
people happy,
and I want
people to feel
good about
themselves in
their rooms.

Blue and white is a classic combination. There's something very appealing about azure-blue raw silk against the chalky white painted finish on my Alexandra chair.

RIGHT: Color and texture and pattern interact to create a whimsical feeling in this sophisticated bedroom for a teenager. The blue chandeliers printed on the curtains, the bed hangings, and the chair provide a strong graphic motif, while the retro shag rug adds a fun element.

I'm always balancing color with a contrast, and often it's white. The white vanity looks very crisp against the glass subway tiles on the bathroom walls. The terrazzo tile on the countertop and floor is embedded with chips of blue that resemble sea glass.

RIGHT: The walls are a tranquil blue, the trim is white, and the curtains carry out the theme with a big blue-and-white stripe. The multicolor rug adds an unexpected burst of energy.

In this bedroom, the walls are painted in Intense Pink from Glidden, and everything else is white—except for the chocolate-brown lamp, which is an unexpected touch. The bed linens bring back all the colors—pink, brown, and white.

RIGHT: Pink and orange work together here because both colors have the same value. The orange sofa and the curtains are trimmed in pink. The burlap-covered walls are outlined in the same pink, in grosgrain ribbon—my favorite trim material. I also used pink and orange grosgrain ribbon to create a pattern on the vintage chair.

When you begin with white, you can introduce other colors in unexpected ways.

The fresh white walls keep the pink from becoming too sweet, because I used the pink everywhere else—even on the ceiling. I found a pair of vintage sofas and then upholstered them in a tweed that reminds me of a classic Chanel suit. You've got to be very brave to go for a pink rug and a bright pink bed. The client's daughter requested a hammock, so we found one that doubles as a guest bed.

PART IV

A SENSE OF PLACE

In the City

IF SOMEONE MENTIONS THAT HE LIVES IN A NEW YORK APARTMENT, we all instantly have a vision in our heads of what that home would look like. I imagine a Park Avenue living room, with antique furniture juxtaposed to contemporary art and a subtle palette in beige and black and taupe. There would be a collection of some intriguing object, like antique tortoiseshell boxes or old architectural fragments, because I think of New Yorkers, and New York, as very sophisticated. Each place has a particular character, and I try to capture something of that when I decorate. But place isn't the only determining factor. The interesting thing is how different two houses in the same city can be.

Each person has his own experience of a place, and his own idea of how he wants to live. A house in the city can be formal or informal, neutral or colorful, full to the brim with furniture or remarkably spare. I have done all sorts of interiors, and the only thing they have in common is that they suit the personalities of the people who live there. I may take a cue from a view out a window or the history of a place, but the real consideration is always the client. I want them to feel as if they belong in this house.

You can see how strong this house is architecturally. When you come into this limestone entrance hall, you're struck by the magnificent proportions, yet it can feel a little cold. I created warmth with an antique rug and a welcoming chair and high-backed upholstered banquettes on either side. A mirrored 1940s Italian screen catches the light. The nineteenth-century pedestal table functions as a room divider between the entrance hall and the living room.

In the city, where I'm not thinking as much about the landscape outside, the biggest influence on my design is the architecture of the house.

The clients have been drawn to this particular style for some reason they may not even be able to define. I want to explore its character with them. This house was constructed by a French builder and those tall doors were actually imported from France. There's an eclectic mix of furniture in the living room—a Biedermeier sofa and chairs, a contemporary, gilded twig table, a leather bergère—as if all these intriguing pieces had been collected over time from various little shops on the Left Bank. A linen panther-patterned carpet holds the three seating groups, and the grand piano, together.

FOLLOWING PAGE: A stunning group of museum-quality antiques creates a symmetrical composition in front of the French doors. The 1830s Austrian library table has an unusual shape that looks beautiful silhouetted against the light. The Dutch antique fluted pedestals echo the columns that flank the entrance to the living room. I love that delicate tassel trim on the late-nineteenth-century French painted side chairs. In the absence of curtains, these pieces act as a sort of stopping point, completing the room.

In a large room,
I always try to
create a range of
seating areas with
different moods.

I built a banquette into a corner to create an island of tranquility, where two people could sit and have a more intimate conversation in the midst of a large group. The chair is an Italian antique; the table is Lucite. I love that mix.

RIGHT: The long, low lines of the contemporary sofa seem to echo the horizontal lines of the moldings. The wall is painted a pale gray-blue, and the pillows pick up the same color, in a deeper shade. There's virtually no pattern on the upholstery. I saved it all for the rug.

This room has the proportions of a ballroom, and I furnished it like a French salon, with chairs that can move wherever you want them. The gilded consoles have turned a darker color of bronze with age. The rug is an antique Agra. The chandelier is fine crystal. In the midst of all this tradition, it's a surprise to see the Elvis screenprint by Russell Young, reflected in the mirror. But it gives the room an edge. Time hasn't stopped. The house will keep changing. It lives.

This room had
a very stark,
graphic look
with thick,
dark window
mullions and a
limestone floor,
and I played up
those strong,
pure lines in the
furniture.

The coffee table is basically two slabs of wood, and
twin stools by Nancy Corzine covered in cognac-
colored leather repeat that strong horizontal. I
brought in more orange with the leather chair
and the Hermès blanket folded over the sofa. The
orange energizes the room, and it's balanced by
the dark chocolate-brown chair that gives weight to
the group. I finished it off with graphic black lamp
shades in front of the two-tone oatmeal curtains.

This library is the definition of urbane. I love those low-slung cognac-colored leather chairs, with a contrast welt in bone leather. The walls are painted a putty color with a dark Russian blue inside the bookcases. If a drawing (or a nineteenth-century Swedish giltwood mirror) doesn't fit on the shelves, just hang it in front. I like the way it breaks up a wall of bookcases.

RIGHT: I added a detail I had seen on antique bookcases—that gilded bead along the shelves and those little wooden numbers. I think you could transport this whole room to the Rue Jacob in Paris—it has that kind of sophistication. The Thornton floor lamp is from my collection for Visual Comfort.

A sofa at the foot of a bed creates a lovely warmth, and makes a bedroom feel like a place you really want to sit and spend time in.

The room is simple and clean, the color palette is fresh, and the curtains are luxurious cashmere in a French silver-blue, a color that is hard to get right. I love how they look against the beautiful white walls, painted in Benjamin Moore's Floral White. White linen upholstery is pure and soothing. I hung an eighteenth-century French carved and gilded panel over the bed and contemporary black-and-white photographs by Rodney Smith on the wall, which makes for a very sophisticated room. The French Empire pier table between the windows is mirrored in the traditional way and reflects the light. I like the topstitching on the wool felt carpet—another couture touch.

This bedroom was conceived as a master suite, and a desk separates the bed from the sitting area. The dark wood furniture is brightened with touches of gilt. I used natural linen to upholster the walls, which adds so much texture and warmth to a large room.

RIGHT: The sitting area opens to its own private terrace—such a treat in the middle of the city. The sofa and chairs are very comfortable, so you can really relax. I like that double row of nail heads on tape, outlining the curves of the Greg Jordan wing chair—it's just the right amount of detail.

In the Country

WHEN CLIENTS ASK ME TO DESIGN A HOUSE in the country for them, I like to visit the site even before the foundation is poured. I want to stand on the property and see what the views will be and where the sun comes up and where you're most likely to get a breeze. In the country, there's a whole different sensitivity to nature than in the city. The natural surroundings have a huge impact on the design, because the house is usually conceived to interact much more with the environment. The boundaries between inside and out blur on loggias, porches, and decks. Many of the family activities take place outside.

A country house is a getaway, a retreat. It's a place to relax and have fun with family and friends. I'll always ask what my clients plan to do in the country. Some people love boating, some love fishing, and it feels very personal to reference that in the design. I might do a room in the colors of a nautical flag, or hang some vintage fish prints on a wall. People feel very connected to a place where they have had good times, and I want the design to have meaning for them. I want to make a place where my clients can create their own memories.

This magnificent window looks directly out at the lake and automatically becomes the focus of the room. I framed it with camel-colored linen curtains, simple enough not to compete, yet with just enough texture and detail to hold their own, thanks to that tasseled trim along the leading edge. It leads your eye up to the beautiful old beams, which are so dramatic. All we did was set them off with white paint on the ceiling and the walls. The furnishings are done in tones of camel and cream and tan and brown, with a touch of blue. The scheme starts with the Rose Tarlow library table, which centers you before you head off into the large room.

This extra-
ordinary log
cabin is a
fascinating mix
of the rustic and
the refined.

Rough-hewn wood and finely carved English Chippendale chairs—I love that contrast. Again, it's that mix of the casual and the dressy that gives such attitude to a room. It shows real confidence. The furniture is upholstered in various patterns and textures that add warmth in winter. In summer, everything is covered in white cotton slipcovers.

RIGHT: That fabulous eighteenth-century painted canvas on the wall sets the mood. It feels almost like a tapestry, and suddenly turns a cabin into an English manor house. The large table under it was designed so it could be pulled into the room and used for dining. I layered the sisal carpet with antique rugs for even more texture and a sense of age. The two eighteenth-century chinoiserie tables in front of the sofa look very chic, and then the antler chandelier brings us back to the country.

FOLLOWING PAGE: When you're in a beautiful place like the South Carolina Low Country, you just want to live outside on the porch. Comfortable rattan chairs are gathered around an octagonal coffee table—more interesting than a square. A circle of chairs is always very conducive to conversation. A long, custom-made table of limestone and iron makes it easy to move a dinner party outside. I chose all the materials for their ability to handle the weather.

This cottage
was designed to
make a guest feel
as if they were
staying in a cozy
little house of
their own.

PREVIOUS PAGE: During the design process, this building evolved to embrace several different uses. It's a retreat where the clients can come and work, but it also functions as a great entertaining space. The walls are more glass than solid, which makes it feel very spacious, and when those industrial-sash doors are open, you can hear the creek running outside. Inside and outside blur, which makes the space ideal for big parties. The furniture is traditional, yet the room has a clean, contemporary look. The ceiling is bare wood, and the floor is made of concrete pavers, layered with rugs for softness.

ABOVE: It's a small-scale space with a very high ceiling. The wing chairs are extra tall, because the room could carry it, and they're upholstered in simple Belgian linen.

RIGHT: One room serves for living, dining, and cooking. It's all done in shades of red, black, and cream to unify the space. Just behind the seating area is a table where you could pull out a laptop, or eat dinner. The kitchen is compact, with open shelves. I took advantage of them, arranging bowls and candlesticks into an attractive display and hanging a sunburst mirror just above to create a focal point.

The cabinet is so large, and the pattern of its glass doors so strong, that in this very simple room it works almost like an architectural element.

The cabinet gives structure to an odd assortment of objects and pulls together whatever you put into it. Random collections look organized. I hung a pair of vintage tennis rackets and antique batik prints on either side to reinforce the symmetry.

In this small space, we hung the beds off the wall on ropes, which makes them almost seem to float.

It feels as if they take up much less space that way, and you have room underneath to store things. Conventional beds pushed up against the windows could have felt cramped. The pillows are finished with rope as well, and I added my favorite Hermès blankets, for a touch of orange. The walls are simple stained pine and all the trim and the doors are painted white. The combination makes me think of a vintage wooden boat, like a Chris-Craft.

The outdoor fireplace is embedded with an old millstone found on the property, and a wooden beam became the mantel. We hung a few iron fish off the side, and that's all the decoration it needs. The beauty is in the weathered textures. The chairs are a contemporary version of the traditional Adirondack chair and tie into that strong, classic aesthetic.

RIGHT: This dining room, just off the porch, has the same feeling. The rattan chairs are very comfortable, so you want to linger around the table. Built-in cabinets add an architectural element, and a lot of storage. I designed a banquette to fit in between the cupboards, with a little table and two chairs. It's a more intimate place for two or three people to sit and dine alone. I painted the ceiling a soft blue-gray between the beams to subtly bring in a color that reappears throughout the house.

Something intriguing happens when you work against type. You might expect a dining room like this in a Georgian house, but not a log cabin.

The client already owned those beautiful English Regency chairs with black-and-gold chinoiserie detailing, and I added the antique table and the Victoria Hagan wing chairs. I'll often put wing chairs at the head and foot of a dining table because they add such presence. These are covered in mustard linen velvet and trimmed with nail heads. The unusual color really makes a statement.

LEFT: Everything in this room is extraordinary. The girandole over the sideboard is a beautifully detailed English Regency piece, crowned with an eagle. A collection of Coalport china dating back to 1798 is arranged on the sideboard. I like the high contrast of fine porcelain and rough-hewn wood.

In the master bedroom, a linen fabric patterned with roses looks as if it, and this new room, have been here forever.

The intricate detailing on the chinoiserie panels is an interesting contrast to the rough walls. The sparkle of crystal and silver adds another dressy note.

RIGHT: The four-poster bed has its own touches of chinoiserie. For the duvet cover, ottoman, and curtains, I used one of my favorite fabrics, a lovely floral from Bennison that has that vintage tea-dyed look. All those roses soften the room. That large rock hanging to the right of the fireplace is actually part of a pulley that lifts up the painting over the fireplace to reveal a TV.

In a country house, I like to take my materials from nature. It makes the rooms feel very connected to the outdoors.

The railing on a stair landing doesn't have to be purely utilitarian. It becomes an art object itself when it's made from branches that form their own organic pattern. A group of framed prints on the wall is more rectilinear, but they share a natural element—they portray pinecones.

RIGHT: In a log cabin, even the four-poster bed is made from logs. White linen, casually tied to the logs, forms a canopy and hangs down to the floor. You get the feeling you could pull it shut to create your own private room within a room. As a finishing touch, I brought in those witty antler stools.

In the butler's pantry, a black Dutch cabinet from the 1850s holds a stunning collection of silver that catches the light. The pieces are casually arranged because they're used every day.

RIGHT: When there are no upper cabinets in a kitchen, it feels more like a room. The countertops and the sink are made of poured concrete, which has a weathered look. You don't have to worry about every spot and stain when the surface already has so much texture. New cabinetry is stained a soft gray-brown to match the old wood. I brought in a lamp, because there's something so cozy about lamplight in a kitchen. Casement windows open wide to let in the breeze.

This is a
country
kitchen, but
it has a clean,
modern edge.

Open shelves, made of stainless steel and set on dark iron brackets, hold dishes and glassware in plain sight. The countertops are made of soapstone, which has a more casual look than granite and enough weight to balance all the white.

RIGHT: The table is antique, and I had the ottomans made at just the right height to serve as bench seating. You almost feel as if you're at a picnic when you're eating a meal here. The brick floor continues outside into the yard, which makes the kitchen feel as if it's part of the outdoors. The room is light and airy.

At the Beach

I LOVE THE LIGHT AT THE BEACH—that pure white light that dissolves the sand and the sea and the sky into one big shimmer. It gives everything it touches a glow. I feel happy at the beach, and as soon as I'm out on the sand, watching the mesmerizing push and pull of the waves and listening to the murmur of the ocean, I am calm. That's the feeling I want to re-create in a beach house. In a second home, there's an opportunity to be bolder, lighter, freer. Released from the obligations of daily life, it's a place where people can really express themselves, where you are suddenly liberated to be the person you want to be. The personality of the house is more relaxed, the furniture more casual. In the bright light at the beach, the colors I use are often more vivid and intense. Pale shades tend to fade away. But I begin, as always, with my signature white. White walls, white slipcovered sofas, whitewashed floors—and then a shot of blue. Isn't that the image of the quintessential beach cottage we all carry around in our heads? That combination is timeless. But I also like the surprise of orange and pink and lavender. You never quite know where all this newfound freedom will lead.

In my own beach house, everything—walls, ceiling, and floor—is painted in Benjamin Moore's White Dove. I start with that white envelope and then I add key accent colors in small ways that make a big statement—like those orange and aqua stripes on my French flea-market chairs. The fabric is Ultrasuede, which is practically indestructible. You can sit on them in a wet bathing suit without a second thought. Instead of hanging the art over the fireplace, I propped it on the mantel to make it more casual. I like to use materials that relate to the setting. The fireplace surround is made of a poured stone embedded with seashells. The coral sconces are a sophisticated way to continue the beach theme.

The corner of the loggia overlooks a walkway to the beach, and the furniture is done in the colors of the sand and the sea. I wanted the house to feel as if it were part of the landscape.

RIGHT: In my beach house, the porch is furnished with a comfortable sofa, where you can sit down with a book or talk to a friend. I even fit in a table and some benches, so you can have an impromptu dinner out here and enjoy the breeze. I incorporated my X-motif into the architecture of the house and it casts the most interesting shadows. The floor is made of the same stone I used on the fireplace. It reminds me of limestone, and then it has the added texture of all the shells.

I spotted these vintage batik prints at a flea market and was attracted to their vivid colors and patterns. I had them framed in bamboo and hung them in a tight grid over the sofa. The effect is multiplied when you see them all together.

When I went looking for pillows, I chose bold patterns in three different colors—orange, green, and blue. The colors all have the same value, which is why they work so well together. The limestone-and-iron coffee table echoes the white and black of the lamps. I found the little round table at a local shop and couldn't resist it since it's made out of seashells.

OPPOSITE: This is really a found space—a landing on the second floor leading to the bedrooms—which I decided to furnish. My daughter and her friends love to hang out here. There's a TV across from the sectional sofa. I fit in two bunk beds for the overflow of guests. We've also had people sleep on the sectional. Blankets and pillows are stored in the ottoman on wheels.

RIGHT: On an afternoon when everybody else is out at the beach, the Archatrive desk is a quiet place to work. It's a simple white plane with X-shaped struts. I added a few touches of orange.

I love blue and white at the beach, and it was fun mixing all these fabrics together.

ABOVE: There's a bright stripe on the curtains, and more blue and white on the pillows that soften the back of the banquette.

LEFT: I built a whole wall of storage in the kitchen. The opaque glass on the cupboard doors turns blue in certain lights, reflecting the dominant color.

OPPOSITE: I had a lamp shade made out of a whimsical print, and hung it over a table. The rattan chairs are very comfortable and add such a great texture. I chose a sophisticated table in a dark finish to contrast with the airiness of the space. It makes the room feel as if the pieces had been collected over time.

ABOVE: This is a secondary family room, so kids and grown-ups can split up, if they like. I added lots of nautical details. The white terrycloth sofa is corded in navy, and the blue and white curtains are attached with rope and grommets.

RIGHT: The two steamer chairs, covered in bright red Ultrasuede, look as if they could have come straight out of the lounge of a 1940s ocean liner. The vintage Louis Vuitton posters pick up the red, white, and blue.

OPPOSITE: The ladder leads to a widow's walk on the roof, where you have a great view of the ocean. I installed the refrigerator and the periwinkle-blue sink so you could make drinks and take them up to watch the sunset.

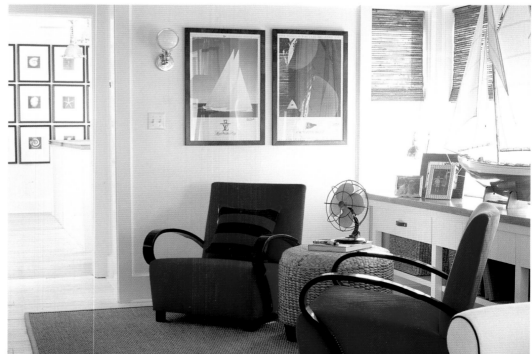

A vintage American flag inspired the colors in this guest room. The three twin beds are made up with denim coverlets and madras pillows. From that classic red leather chair at the window, you can watch the boats sail by.

RIGHT: I found antique nautical flags and hung them in the bathroom to create this bright, graphic pattern. The hanging lanterns add to the marine feel. The vanity is painted navy blue with a stainless-steel counter.

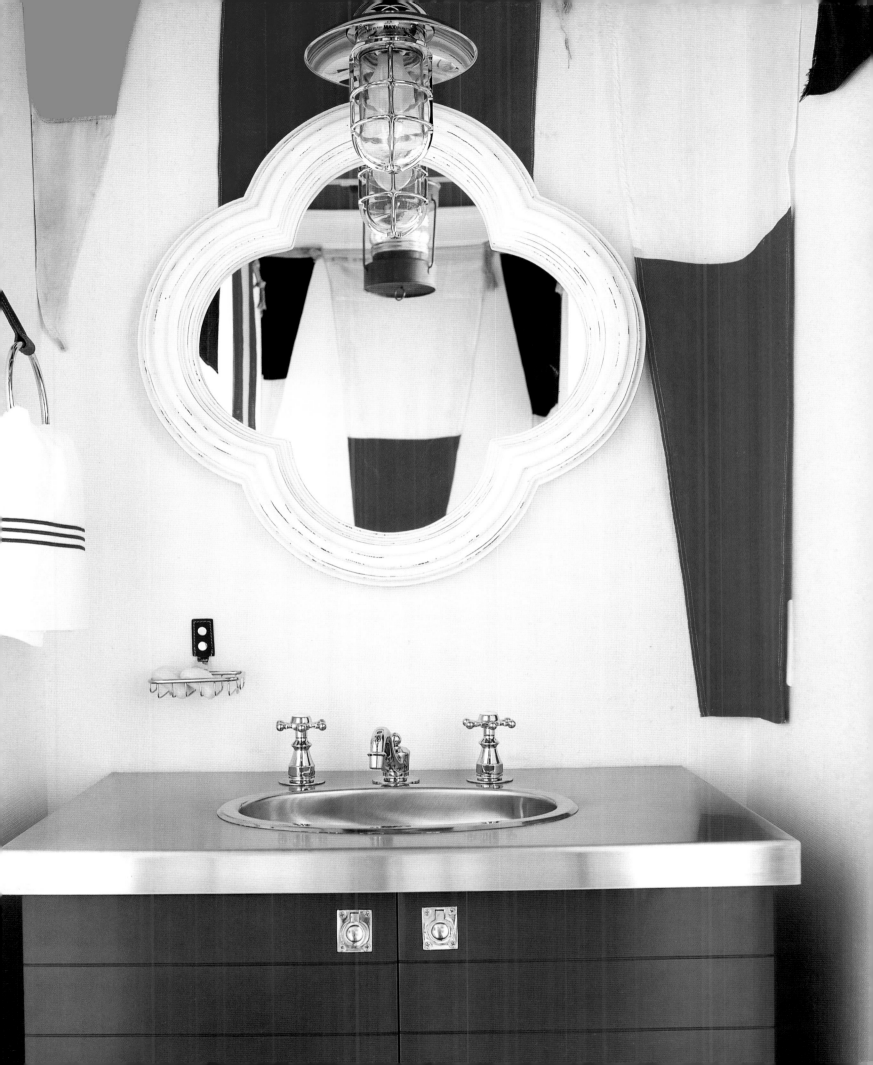

It feels like summer camp in this guest room under the eaves.

LEFT: The seven beds are all made up in colorful cotton comforters. With all those vibrant patterns on the beds—and the floor, with striped cotton rugs— I kept the walls very plain, in pure, crisp white.

I found an old-fashioned industrial sink and hung buckets on the wall for toiletries. The kids in the extended family love it up here. They can all be together.

Stripes are a classic motif at the beach. You need strong colors that can stand up to the intense light.

This little beach cabana and matching chair from Janus et Cie all fold up at the end of the day. I like a vivid stripe, because it really comes to life in this light.

RIGHT: That Etro beach towel laid over a chaise was my inspiration for this porch. I found a striped cotton fabric in the same colors and made it into pillows. The rattan chairs are very flexible—they can move together as a sectional or split apart. Each one has cushions trimmed in a different color to match the pillows—green, turquoise, orange, or pink. That small touch has a large impact.

The colors in this master bedroom are taken from coral and conch shells and sand. I lacquered a screen in a dusty shell pink and set it behind a headboard upholstered in white linen and draped with a linen throw. That layering of texture and color continues throughout the room and makes it feel softer and more luxurious.

RIGHT: I made my own stripe out of pink and taupe and white and used it as a border on the curtains. It's a dressmaker detail that adds individuality and pulls together all the colors in the room. The walls are painted in Rice Grain and the trim is White Flour, both by Sherwin-Williams.

Anything can become an intriguing display. These are inexpensive wood brackets topped with coral, which becomes very sculptural when it's featured this way.

It wouldn't have had the same impact if I only had one or two. When it comes to displaying a collection, quantity is key. I love the white-on-white effect—white brackets, white coral, white walls, white floors—and then the dark contrast of the bedside chests and bench. To finish it off, I added lavender lamps. It's a color you don't expect, which makes it even more beautiful.

I wanted to capture that scintillating light that plays off the water. Everything in this sunroom seems to shimmer.

The Niermann Weeks folding screens are made of watery, antiqued mirror, and my Loring cocktail table for Hickory Chair is reverse-painted glass. Fortuny fabric, draped over the custom-made, high-backed sofa, adds another layer of tone-on-tone yellow and gold. Swedish chairs from the 1880s are done in the same palette. The sunburst mirror is painted white, and the walls are done in Benjamin Moore's Sage Tint, with a trellis frieze in Benjamin Moore's White Dove along the ceiling. This is a historic house in Palm Beach, and it deserved to be a little dressier than the typical beach cottage.

The New Eighteenth-Century Style
ANDRE ARBUS

Design Resources

There are so many wonderful design resources for home furnishings. These shops and companies are a few of my favorites.

Ainsworth Noah and Associates
351 Peachtree Hills Avenue, Suite 515
Atlanta, Georgia 30305
404.231.8787
www.ainsworth-noah.com

Amy Perlin Antiques
206 East 61st Street, 4th Floor
New York, New York 10065
212.593.5756
www.amyperlinantiques.com

Angie Tyner
200 Bennett Street NW
Atlanta, Georgia 30309
404.367.4484
www.swedishantiques.biz

Anthropologie
30 Industrial Park Boulevard
Trenton, South Carolina 29847
800.309.2500
www.anthropologie.com

Belvedere
996 Huff Road NW
Atlanta, Georgia 30318
404.352.1942
www.belvedereinc.com

Bill Lowe Gallery
1555 Peachtree Street NE, Suite 100
Atlanta, Georgia 30309
404.352.8114
www.lowegallery.com

Bradley Hughes
652 Miami Circle
Atlanta, Georgia 30324
404.814.9595
www.bradley-hughes.com

Bungalow
1197 Howell Mill Road NW
Atlanta, Georgia 30318
www.bungalowclassic.com
404.351.9120

Dennis & Leen/Formations
8720 Melrose Avenue
West Hollywood, California 90069
310.652.0855
www.dennisandleen.com

Dwellings
210 11th Avenue, Suite 300
New York, New York 10001
212.717.5753
www.dwellingshome.com

Edgar Reeves
425 Peachtree Hills Avenue, Suite 16
Atlanta, Georgia 30305
404.237.1137
www.edgar-reeves.com

Hermès, Paris
24, rue du Faubourg Saint-Honoré
75008 Paris, France
33.1.40.17.47.17
www.hermes.com

Hollyhock
817 Hilldale Avenue
West Hollywood, California 90069
323.931.3400
www.hollyhockinc.com

Hyman Hendler Ribbon
21 West 38th Street, Suite B
New York, New York 10018
212.840.8393
www.hymanhendler.com

Interiors Market
55 Bennett Street NW, Suite 20
Atlanta, Georgia 30309
404.352.0055
www.interiorsmarket.com

Jackson Fine Art
3115 East Shadowlawn Avenue NE
Atlanta, Georgia 30305
404.233.3739
www.jacksonfineart.com

Jane J. Marsden Antiques and Interiors
2300 Peachtree Road NW,
Suite A102
Atlanta, Georgia 30309
404.355.1288
www.marsdenantiques.com

Jerry Pair Touring
351 Peachtree Hills Avenue, Suite 508
Atlanta, Georgia 30305
404.261.6337
www.jerrypair.com

Lars Bolander Shop
72 Ganesvoort Street
New York, New York 10014
212.924.1000
www.larsbolander.com

LIEF
646 North Almont Drive
Los Angeles, California 90069
310.492.0033

Mansour Modern
8606 Melrose Avenue
West Hollywood, California 90069
310.652.1121
www.mansourmodern.com

Mecox Gardens
962 Lexington Avenue
New York, New York 10021
212.249.5301
www.mecoxgardens.com

Moattar
351 Peachtree Hills Avenue, Suite 314
Atlanta, Georgia 30305
404.237.5100
www.moattar.com

Nancy Corzine, Palm Beach
375 S. County Road
Palm Beach, Florida 33480
561.820.1501
www.nancycorzine.com

Nicholson Gallery
764 Miami Circle NE, Suite 136
Atlanta, Georgia 30324
www.thenicholsongallery.
gtengineers.com
404.848.9553

Parc Monceau
425 Peachtree Hills Avenue NE
Atlanta, Georgia 30305
404.467.8107
www.parcmonceauatl.com

Paris Flea Market
www.parispuces.com

Persian Galleries
2860 Piedmont Road
Atlanta, Georgia 30305
404.261.8888
www.persiangalleries.com

Pierce Martin
99 Armour Drive NE
Atlanta, Georgia 30305
404.872.0800
www.piercemartin.com

Richard Shapiro
8905 Melrose Avenue
West Hollywood, California 90069
310.275.6700

Ritz Paris
15, Place Vendôme
75001 Paris, France
33.1.43.16.30.30
www.ritzparis.com

Robuck & Co. Antiques
425 Peachtree Hills Avenue NE,
Suite 20
Atlanta, Georgia 30305
404.351.7173
www.robuckandcompany.com

Rogers & Goffigon Ltd.
41 Chestnut Street
Greenwich, Connecticut 06830
203.532.8068

Rose Tarlow Melrose House
8454 Melrose Place
Los Angeles, California 90069
323.651.2202
www.rosetarlow.com

Saladino
200 Lexington Avenue, Suite 1600
New York, New York 10016
212.684.3720
www.saladinostyle.com

Stalls at Bennett Street
116 Bennett Street NW
Atlanta, Georgia 30309
404.352.4430
www.thestalls.com

Stark Carpet
979 Third Avenue
New York, New York 10022
212.752.9000
www.starkcarpet.com

Travis & Co.
351 Peachtree Hills Avenue NE,
Suite 128
Atlanta, Georgia 30305
404.237.5079
www.travisandcompany.com

Willard Pitt Curtainmakers
2144 Hills Avenue NW
Atlanta, Georgia 30318
404.355.8232

William Word
707 Miami Circle NE
Atlanta, Georgia 30324
404.233.6890
www.williamwordantiques.com

www.1stdibs.com

My Collections:

Hickory Chair
P.O. Box 2147
Hickory, North Carolina 28603
828.328.1802
www.hickorychair.com

Lee Jofa
979 Third Avenue, Suite 234
New York, New York 10022
212.688.0444
www.leejofa.com

Safavieh
238 East 59th Street
New York, New York 10022
212.888.7847
www.safavieh.com

Soicher-Marin
12824 Cerise Avenue
Hawthorne, California 90250
310.679.5000
www.soicher-marin.com

Visual Comfort
Circa Lighting
2021 Bingle Road
Houston, Texas 77055
317.686.5999
www.visualcomfort.com

Architects featured in this book:

Cooper, Robertson & Partners
311 West 43rd Street
New York, New York 10036
212.247.1717
www.cooperrobertson.com

Jack Davis
425 Peachtree Hills Avenue NE,
Suite 31B
Atlanta, Georgia 30305
404.237.2333

Evans Woollen
Woollen, Molzan & Partners
600 Kentucky Avenue, Suite 101
Indianapolis, Indiana 46225
317.632.7484

Harrison Design Associates
3198 Cains Hill Place NW
Atlanta, Georgia 30305
404.365.7760
www.harrisondesignassociates.com

Kenward Architectural Studio
425 Peachtree Hills Avenue, Suite 21C
Atlanta, Georgia 30305
404.814.0277

Spitzmiller & Norris
5825 Glenridge Drive NE, Suite 1-206
Sandy Springs, Georgia 30328
404.843.3874
www.spitzmillerandnorris.com

Summerour and Associates
409 Bishop Street NW
Atlanta, Georgia 30318
404.603.8585
www.summerour.net

William T. Baker & Associates
78 West Wesley Road NW
Atlanta, Georgia 30305
404.261.0446
www.wtbaker.com

Photography Credits

Quentin Bacon: page 118 (bottom)

beall+thomas photography: pages 40, 42, 43, 45, 152 (top, right; bottom, right) 174, 175, 176, 178, 180, 181, 188, 189, 190, 191, 193, 194, 195, 196, 197, 212, 213

Cheryl Dalton: pages 96 (bottom, right), 106, 109, 138, 139

Erica George Dines Photography: pages 6 (top, left), 7, 9, 10 (top, right; middle, right), 24 (top, middle; middle, right), 32, 44, 84, 85, 86, 88, 89, 90, 96 (bottom, left), 100, 199, 202, 204, 205, 218

Colleen Duffley Photography: pages 152 (middle, left), 201

Emily J. Followill: page 152 (top, left)

Tria Giovan: pages 6 (bottom, right), 7 (middle, right), 56, 64, 66, 67, 68, 69, 80, 96 (top, left), 102, 120 (top), 121, 127, 128, 143, 152 (middle, right; bottom, left), 162, 163, 173, 186, 187, 192, 210; courtesy of Benjamin Moore & Co.: 17, 18, 19, 119; courtesy of *Veranda*: 220; reprinted with permission from Meredith Corporation. © 2009 Meredith Corporation. All rights reserved: 24 (top, left; middle, left), 38, 39, 55, 110, 111, 152 (top, middle); reprinted with permission from *Southern Accents.* © 2004: 63, 131, 132, 134, 135, 146, 147, 182, 184, 200, 206, 207 (top; bottom), 208 (top; bottom), 209, 211, 214, 215, 216, 217

John Grover: pages 118 (top); courtesy of *Veranda*: 48, 49, 50, 99, 142

Josh Hollar, courtesy of Hickory Chair: page 114

Hilary Hurt: page 10 (center)

Frances Janisch: pages 6 (middle, left), 24 (bottom, left), 75, 76, 79, 92, 93, 94

Thibault Jeanson, courtesy of *Veranda*: pages 6 (bottom, left), 24 (center), 36, 37, 82, 83, 96 (middle, left; center), 120 (bottom), 155, 156, 158, 160, 161, 164, 166, 167, 168

Jeff McNamara: pages 62, 72, 73, 96 (bottom, middle), 108

Pamela Mougin: page 152 (center)

Emily Minton Redfield: pages 104, 117

Kenton Robertson Photography © 2009: pages 7 (middle, left; bottom, right), 113, 122, 123, 124 (bottom), 125, 144

Philip Shone: page 96 (top, right)

Suzanne Kasler Interiors: page 96 (middle, right)

Peter Vitale: pages 47; courtesy of *Veranda*: 6 (middle, right), 24 (bottom, middle), 58, 59, 60

Simon Watson: cover and pages 7 (top, right), 31, 53, 70, 71, 136, 140, 145, 148, 150

Janie Wilburn: pages 10 (top, left), 124 (top; right)

William Waldron: pages 2, 5, 6 (top, right), 7 (top, left), 10 (bottom, left; bottom, right), 13, 14, 20, 22, 23, 24 (bottom, right), 27, 28, 34, 35, 46, 51, 149, 170, 171

First published in the United States of America in 2009 by Rizzoli International Publications, Inc.
300 Park Avenue South
New York, New York 10010
www.rizzoliusa.com

Text copyright © 2009 Suzanne Kasler

2010 2011 2012 2013 / 10 9 8 7 6 5 4

PRINTED IN CHINA

ISBN 13: 978-0-8478-3220-0

Library of Congress Control Number 2001012345

Project Editor: Sandra Gilbert
Art Direction: Doug Turshen with David Huang

Front.

Back.

nail heads

Detail.

my detail